MACHINE LEARNING INTERVIEW

Questions & Answers

100+ questions with explanation

First Edition

Aditya Chatterjee   Geoffrey Ziskovin

1

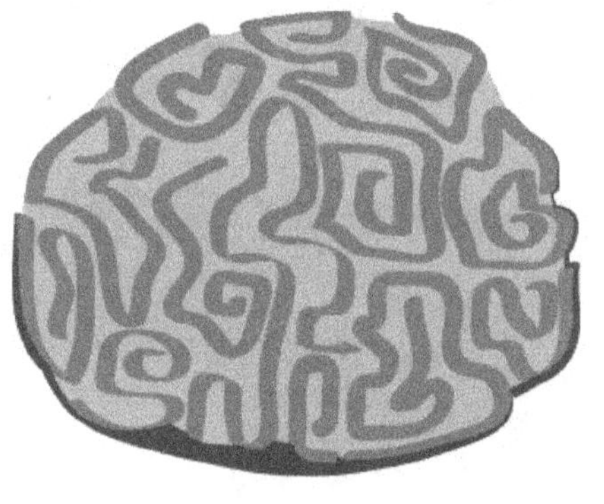

INTRODUCTION

This book **"Machine Learning Interview Questions & Answers"** is a must practice book to test your knowledge in the field of Machine Learning.

The field is vast and Industry takes a different approach. The questions are tailored specific to the Industry Interviews which tests your theoretical knowledge of the field relevant for practical work.

This book has over 120 MCQs (Multiple Choice Questions). Each one is provided with the correct answer along with in-depth explanation. So, your revision will be complete as you attempt the problems.

This includes core questions from Deep Learning important for ML Interviews as well.

This book covers all core topics through the carefully selected set of Interview Questions:

- Core ML techniques like Classification, Regression, Clustering
- Core ML concepts like Supervised, Unsupervised and Semi-Supervised Learning, Naive Bayes,

Central Limit Theorem, Standardization and much more.

- DL concepts relevant for ML Interviews like CNN, RNN, fundamental operations like Fully Connected Layer and much more.

One must go through this book at regular intervals to test their knowledge and identify loopholes in their understanding so that it can be corrected in time.

Book: Machine Learning Interview Questions & Answers

Authors (2): Aditya Chatterjee, Geoffrey Ziskovin

About the authors:

- **Aditya Chatterjee** is an Independent Researcher, Technical Author and the Founding Member of OPENGENUS, a scientific community focused on Computing Technology.
- **Geoffrey Ziskovin** is an American Software Engineer with an experience of over 30 years. He has interviewed over 700 candidates worldwide for various Fortune 500 companies.

Contributors (2): Benjamin QoChuk: Computer Science Researcher, Inventor and Software Developer; **Leandro Baruch**: IT Project Services Specialist at UNHCR (UN Refugee Agency)

Published: May 2022 (Edition 1)

Publisher: © OpenGenus

ISBN: 9798816981644

Contact: team@opengenus.org

Available on Amazon as Paperback & Hardcover.

Table of Contents

Recommended Books

- <u>Linked List Problems</u>: For Interviews and Competitive Programming
- <u>Problems on Array</u>
- <u>Binary Tree Problems</u>
- <u>Dynamic Programming on Trees</u>

- <u>Day before Coding Interview</u> series
- <u>#7daysOfAlgo</u> series

Machine Learning Interview Questions

In this chapter, we have presented Multiple Choice Questions (MCQs) in core Machine Learning topics with a focus on Interviews. Each question has been provided with the correct answer along with detailed explanation.

By practicing these questions, you will get prepared on the following Machine Learning topics:

- Supervised, Unsupervised and Semi-Supervised Learning
- Naive Bayes, Central Limit Theorem, Regularization, Standardization, Normalization, Overfitting, Underfitting, Gradient descent, Backpropagation, K nearest neighbor algorithm

- Distance metrics, Clustering, Classification, Regression

Q1. Which one of the following does not use Labeled Data for Training?

a) Supervised Learning

b) Unsupervised Learning

c) Semi-Supervised Learning

Answer: b) Unsupervised Learning

Unsupervised Learning use only Unlabeled data for Training. In short, the idea is as follows:

- Supervised Learning: Labeled Data only
- Unsupervised Learning: Unlabeled Data only
- Semi-Supervised Learning: Combination of Labeled and Unlabeled Data

---

Q2. Supervised Learning is classified as Regression and Classification. Which one of the following is an example of Classification?

a) Linear Regression

b) Polynomial Regression

c) Logistic Regression

d) Non-Linear Regression

Answer: c) Logistic Regression

In Logistic Regression, the answer is either 0 or 1. Hence, it is used for Classification. The other types are examples of Regression.

Supervised Learning is of two types:

- Regression

- Classification

Regression include techniques like:

- Linear Regression
- Bayesian Linear Regression
- Polynomial Regression
- Regression Trees

Classification include techniques like:

- Decision Tree
- Random Forest
- Logistic Regression
- Support Vector Machine

Q3. Like Supervised Learning, Unsupervised Learning is of two types as well. What are the two types?

a) Regression

b) Clustering

c) Composition

d) Association

Answer: b) Clustering and d) Association

Unsupervised Learning is of two types:

- Clustering
- Association

Clustering is the technique of grouping data while Association is the technique of finding relation between variables in a dataset (for Recommendation applications).

Q4. Which one of the following is an example of Semi-Supervised Learning?

a) Linear Regression

b) Logistic Regression

c) K means Clustering

d) Generative Adversarial Network (GAN)

Answer: d. Generative Adversarial Network (GAN)

Semi-Supervised Learning is a technique that makes use of both Labeled and Unlabeled data. GAN is an example of Semi-Supervised Learning.

In fact, GAN can be used as Unsupervised, Semi-Supervised and Fully-Supervised Learning. GAN models are used to generate a new set of data based on the input data. In contrast, Linear and Logistic Regression can be used as Supervised Learning only while K means Clustering is used as Unsupervised Learning.

Q5. Standard ML applications like Image Recognition is an example of?

a) Supervised Learning

b) Unsupervised Learning

c) Semi-Supervised Learning

Answer: a) Supervised Learning

Standard ML applications like Image Recognition require trained models like ResNet50 which are examples of Supervised Learning as the training data are labeled.

Q6. In Naive Bayes classifier equation, what is P(A|B)?

a) Likelihood of evidence given hypothesis is true

b) Posterior probability of hypothesis given evidence is true

c) Prior probability of hypothesis

d) Prior probability that evidence is true

Answer: b) Posterior probability of hypothesis given evidence is true

Naive Bayes classifier equation is as follows:

P(A|B) = P(B|A) P(A) / P(B)

The different terms are as follows:

- Likelihood of evidence given hypothesis is true: P(B|A)
- Posterior probability of hypothesis given evidence is true: P(A|B)
- Prior probability of hypothesis: P(A)
- Prior probability that evidence is true: P(B)

Q7. Naive Bayes classifier is an example of?

a) Low Bias, Low Variance

b) High Bias, Low Variance

c) Low Bias, High Variance

d) High Bias, High Variance

Answer: b) High Bias, Low Variance

Naive Bayes classifier is an example of High Bias, Low Variance.

If the training data is small and the number of features is high, then High Bias and Low Variance algorithms are used. Examples include Linear SVM and Naive Bayes classifier.

If training data is large, then Low Bias and High Variance algorithm is used such as K Nearest neighbors, Decision Tree, Random forest.

Q8. In Central Limit Theorem, as data size becomes large, the distribution becomes?

a) Poisson Distribution

b) Binomial Distribution

c) Normal distribution

d) Cannot be determined

Answer: c) Normal distribution

Central Limit Theorem states that as data size becomes large, the distribution of the data becomes Normal distribution.

In other terms, if the sample data is large, then the mean of the sample data will be very close to the actual mean of the entire data set.

Q9. How many types of Regularization techniques are there?

---

a) 4

b) 6

c) 10

d) 2

Answer: d) 2

There are two types of Regularization namely:

- L1 Regularization (Lasso)
- L2 Regularization (Ridge)

Q10. The difference in L1 and L2 Regularization is in?

a) Beta term

b) Lambda

c) Penalty term

d) Loss function

Answer: c) Penalty term

The difference in L1 and L2 Regularization is in Penalty term.

Following is the equation of L1 Regularization:

$$\sum_{i=1}^{n}\left(y_i - \beta_0 - \sum_{j=1}^{p}\beta_j x_{ij}\right)^2 + \lambda\sum_{j=1}^{p}|\beta_j| = \text{RSS} + \lambda\sum_{j=1}^{p}|\beta_j|.$$

Following is the equation of L2 Regularization:

$$\sum_{i=1}^{n}\left(y_i - \beta_0 - \sum_{j=1}^{p}\beta_j x_{ij}\right)^2 + \lambda\sum_{j=1}^{p}\beta_j^2 = \text{RSS} + \lambda\sum_{j=1}^{p}\beta_j^2$$

Q11. To prevent Overfitting, data is split into how many parts?

12

---

a) 2

b) 3

c) 4

d) 5

Answer: b) 3

Overfitting is the problem where a model learns the low-level features more accurately compared to high level features of the training data. Due to this, the trained model performs with near 100% accuracy for training data but low accuracy for another dataset.

To prevent Overfitting, one approach is to split the data into 3 parts namely:

- Training set
- Cross validation
- Test set
-

Q12. If a model is trained using K nearest neighbor algorithm, underfitting will most likely happen for which value of K?

a) 1

b) 2

c) 5

d) 20

Answer: d) 20

Larger the value of K, the more likely underfitting will take place.

Similarly, the smaller the value of K, the more likely overfitting will take place.

Hence, it is very important to use the correct value of K in K nearest neighbor algorithm and this is a challenge as well.

Q13. Among the two, which one is more likely to result in underfitting?

a) Decision tree

b) Decision stump

Answer: b) Decision stump

As a rule, Decision stump is more likely to result in underfitting while Decision tree is more likely to result in overfitting. Hence, the behavior of both is opposite with respect to overfitting and underfitting.

Q14. In case of overfitting, the training error is _______ compared to test error?

a) Less

b) Equal

c) Greater

Answer: a) Less

In case of overfitting, the model is well versed with the training dataset and hence, the error is least in case of training dataset. Therefore, the training error is less compared to test error.

Ideally, models should be training such that:

- train error is as close as test error as possible
- error should be minimal

Q15. In case of overfitting, the model will most likely have?

a) High variance

b) High bias

Answer: a) High variance

Overfitting results in high variance while underfitting results in High bias.

Q16. Gradient descent is an optimization algorithm to find local minimum of a differentiable function. Gradient descent take steps in _______ direction of gradient?

a) Positive

b) Negative

c) Maximum change

Answer: b) Negative

Gradient descent take steps in negative direction of gradient. This enables Gradient descent to take a steep descent and reach the local minimum.

Q17. Which one of the following is computationally fastest?

a) Batch gradient descent

b) Mini-batch gradient descent

c) Stochastic gradient descent

Answer: c) Stochastic gradient descent

The idea is as follows:

- Batch gradient descent consider the entire dataset to take a single step
- Mini-batch gradient descent considers a small batch from the dataset to take a single step.

- Stochastic gradient descent considers only one data point to take a single step

Q18. When no hyper-parameter is present, which one will you use?

a) Stochastic gradient descent

b) Ordinary Least Squares

Answer: b) Ordinary Least Squares

Ordinary Least Squares does not require hyper-parameters but Stochastic gradient descent do. These differences are:

- Time Complexity of Stochastic gradient descent is $O(K N^2)$ while for Ordinary Least Squares, it is $O(N^3)$.
- Stochastic gradient descent require hyper-parameters but Ordinary Least Squares do not.

- Stochastic gradient descent need to iterate but Ordinary Least Squares do not.

Q19. Momentum gradient descent is used over Stochastic and mini-batch gradient descent to overcome a specific problem. What is the problem?

a) Oscillation

b) Non-linear

c) Learning rate

Answer: a) Oscillation

Oscillation is the problem that parameter of a model is updated with every step but the direction of update involve some variance in gradient steps. To overcome oscillation, Momentum gradient descent is used over Stochastic and mini-batch gradient descent.

Q20. Gradient descent can be applied on both convex and non-convex function. What is the main feature of non-convex function?

a) Only one minimum value

b) More than one minimum value

c) Monotonic increasing function

d) Monotonic decreasing function

Answer: b) More than one minimum value

Convex function has only one minimum value which is the global minimum but in case of non-convex function, there are multiple minimum value so there are many local minima and one global minima.

Q21. Perceptron is an example of?

a) Association

b) Binary classifier

c) Clustering

Answer: b) Binary classifier

Perceptron is an example of Binary classifier which is a type of Supervised learning.

Q22. What are the limitations of Backpropagation?

a) Slow convergence

b) Scaling

c) Local minima problem

d) Oscillation

Answer: a, b, c

The limitations of Backpropagation are:

- Slow convergence
- Scaling
- Local minima problem

Q23. How does learning is stopped in Backpropagation?

a) Learning rate

b) Gradient value

c) Heuristic condition

Answer: b) Gradient value

In case of Backpropagation, learning process is stopped where the average value of gradient goes below a certain threshold value.

Q24. Which algorithm is used in Backpropagation?

a) Gradient descent

b) Activation function

c) Naive Bayes classifier

Answer: a) Gradient descent

Gradient descent is used in Backpropagation. Backpropagation is the most important operation for training a Machine Learning model and Gradient descent helps in reaching minima to minimize training error.

This is a computational expensive operation. This was the reason why Machine Learning was not popular in 1980s despite the fact that the field was mature theoretically. In 2010s, with the introduction of powerful computing devices, Machine Learning became feasible and took a big leap.

Q25. Which one of the following distance metrics is used for categorical variable in K nearest neighbor algorithm?

a) Manhattan distance

b) Euclidean distance

c) Hamming distance

Answer: c) Hamming distance

Hamming distance is used for categorical data while the other two metrics namely

Manhattan and Euclidean distance are used for continuous data.

Q26. In K nearest neighbor algorithm, the value of K is chosen where?

a) Distance between clusters in maximized

b) Validation error is minimum

c) Based on experimentation

Answer: b) Validation error is minimum

In K nearest neighbor algorithm, the value of K is chosen where Validation error is minimum. This improves the accuracy of the algorithm.

Q27. Which of the following can be used to predict missing values in continuous and categorical data?

---

a) Linear regression

b) Polynomial regression

c) K nearest neighbor

Answer: c) K nearest neighbor

K nearest neighbor is used with both continuous and categorical data whereas Regression techniques work with continuous data only. All three techniques can be used to predict missing values in the data they are applied on.

Q28. Euclidean distance is a special case of?

a) Manhattan distance

b) Chebyshev Distance

c) Minkowski distance

Answer: c) Minkowski distance

Euclidean distance is a special case of Minkowski distance where $p = 2$. Furthermore, Manhattan distance is also a special case of Minkowski distance where $p = 1$.

Consider two points P_1 and P_2:

P_1: $(X_1, X_2, ..., X_N)$

P_2: $(Y_1, Y_2, ..., Y_N)$

Then, the Minkowski distance between P_1 and P_2 is given as:

Distance $= [(X_1-Y_1)^P + (X_2-Y_2)^P + ... + (X_N-Y_N)^P]^{(1/P)}$

With P = 2, we get Euclidean distance.

With P = 1, we get Manhattan distance.

Q29. What will be the Euclidean distance between two points (1, 2) and (5, 5)?

a) 7

b) 5

c) 1

d) 4

Answer: b) 5

Euclidean distance = $[(x_1 - x_2)^2 + (y_1 - y_2)^2]^{0.5}$

So, the calculation is as follows:

$[(1-5)^2 + (2-5)^2]^{0.5}$

$= [(-4)^2 + (-3)^2]^{0.5}$

$= [16+9]^{0.5}$

$= 25^{0.5}$

$= 5$

Q30. What will be the Manhattan distance between two points (1, 2) and (5, 5)?

a) 7

b) 5

c) 1

d) 4

Answer: a) 7

Manhattan distance $= [|x_1 - x_2| + |y_1 - y_2|]$

where $|x|$ is mod of x.

So, the calculation is as follows:

$[|1-5| + |2-5|]$

$= [|-4| + |-3|]$

$= [4 + 3]$

= 7

Q31. What will be the Chebyshev distance between two points (1, 2) and (5, 5)?

a) 7

b) 5

c) 1

d) 4

Answer: d) 4

Chebyshev Distance = Maximum($|x_1 - x_2|$, $|y_1 - y_2|$)

So, the calculation is as follows:

Maximum($|1-5|$, $|2-5|$)

= Maximum($|-4|$, $|-3|$)

= Maximum(4, 3)

= 4

This image summarizes the distance metrics:

Euclidean Distance	Manhattan Distance	Chebyshev Distance
$\sqrt{(x_1 - x_2)^2 + (y_1 - y_2)^2}$	$\lvert x_1 - x_2\rvert + \lvert y_1 - y_2\rvert$	$\max(\lvert x_1 - x_2\rvert , \lvert y_1 - y_2\rvert)$

Q32. Clustering is a type of?

a) Supervised

b) Unsupervised

Answer: b) Unsupervised

Clustering is the technique of grouping data and hence, does not require labeled data. In fact, clustering is one of the two types of

32

Unsupervised Learning. Unsupervised Learning is of two types:

- Clustering
- Association

Q33. What is the minimum number of features required for Clustering?

a) 0

b) 1

c) 2

d) 3

Answer: b) 1

The minimum number of features required for Clustering is 1. The data is clustered based on the input feature.

Q34. Does the output of K-means Clustering remain same across different runs?

a) Yes

b) No

Answer: b) No

The output of K means Clustering vary across different runs. This is because K means Clustering go to a local minima and not the global minima. Due to this, it can land to different local minima for each run.

Q35. Which clustering algorithm have the problem of convergence at local optima?

a) K means clustering algorithm

b) Diverse clustering algorithm

---

c) Agglomerative clustering algorithm

d) Expectation Maximization clustering algorithm

Answer: a) K means clustering algorithm, d) Expectation Maximization clustering algorithm

Only two clustering algorithms have the problem of convergence at local optima. These are K means clustering algorithm and Expectation Maximization clustering algorithm.

Q36. Which Clustering algorithm has the problem of outlier?

a) K medoids clustering algorithm

b) K means clustering algorithm

c) K medians clustering algorithm

d) K modes clustering algorithm

Answer: b) K means clustering algorithm

Only K means clustering algorithm has the problem of outlier. This is because it considers the mean of data points of a cluster.

Q37. In this graph of Silhouette coefficient vs Number of clusters, which one of the best number of clusters?

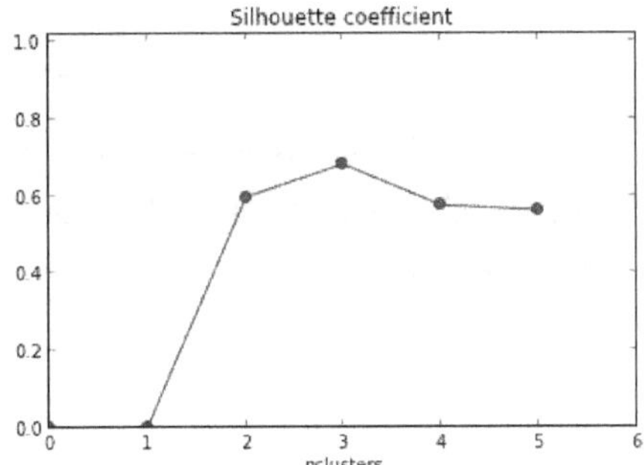

a) 2

b) 3

c) 4

d) 5

Answer: b) 3

Silhouette coefficient is a metric of how similar an object is to its own cluster compared to other clusters. Higher the Silhouette coefficient, the better is the clustering.

For the number of clusters = 3, Silhouette coefficient is the highest and hence, it is the best number of clusters.

Q38. Which one is an iterative technique to handle missing values before Clustering Analysis?

a) Imputation with mean

b) Nearest Neighbor assignment

c) Imputation with median

d) Imputation with Expectation Maximization algorithm

Answer: d) Imputation with Expectation Maximization algorithm

All the four techniques can be used to handle missing values before Clustering Analysis but only one technique namely "Imputation with Expectation Maximization algorithm" is an iterative technique.

Q39. F-Score is used to measure Clustering result. What is the range of F-Score?

a) [0, 100]

b) [-1, 1]

c) [0, 1]

d) All possible values

Answer: c) [0, 1]

F-Score value can range from 0 to 1.

- 1 denotes correct cluster has been assigned.
- 0 denotes that the value of precession and recall is 0

Q40. What one of the Clustering algorithm involve a Merging step?

a) K means clustering

---

b) Mean Shift Clustering Algorithm

c) Hierarchical Clustering

d) DBSCAN Clustering Algorithm

Answer: c) Hierarchical Clustering

Hierarchical Clustering involve merging as the last step while forming clusters. If iteration is not stopped, then only one cluster remain at the end.

Q41. K means algorithm is non-deterministic. Hierarchical Clustering is?

a) Deterministic

b) Non-deterministic

Answer: a) Deterministic

Unlike K means clustering algorithm, Hierarchical Clustering is a deterministic clustering technique that is the result remain the same across different iterations.

Q42. What is the method called which is used to measure distance between two clusters?

a) Linkage method

b) Distance metric

c) F-Score

Answer: a) Linkage method

There are many ways to determine the distance between two clusters (aka linkage methods):

- Single linkage: the distance between two clusters is defined as the minimum value of all pairwise distances between the elements of the first cluster and elements of the second cluster.
- Complete linkage: the distance between two clusters is defined as the maximum value of all pairwise distances between the elements of the first cluster and elements of the second cluster.
- Average linkage: the distance between two clusters is defined as the average distance between the elements of the first cluster and elements of the second cluster.
- Centroid linkage: the distance between two clusters is defined as the distance between the centroids of the two clusters.

Q43. What is the main disadvantage of K means clustering algorithm?

a) Non-deterministic nature

b) Initialization of centroid

c) Value of K

Answer: b) Initialization of centroid

The main drawback of k-means algorithm is that it is very much dependent on the initialization of the centroids or the mean points.

In this way, if a centroid is introduced to be a "far away" point, it may very well wind up without any data point related with it and simultaneously more than one cluster may wind up connected with a solo centroid. Likewise, more than one centroid may be introduced into a similar group bringing about poor clustering.

Q44. What is the Time Complexity of Mean Shift Clustering Algorithm?

a) O(N)

---

b) $O(N^2)$

c) $O(N^{0.5})$

d) $O(\log N)$

Answer: b) $O(N^2)$

The Mean Shift clustering algorithm can be computationally expensive for large datasets, because we have to iteratively follow our procedure for each data point.

It has a time complexity of $O(N^2)$, where n is the number of data points.

Q45. In Mean Shift Clustering Algorithm, for which value of bandwidth will convergence be missed?

a) Too high

---

b) Too low

c) 0

Answer: b) Too low

For Mean Shift Clustering Algorithm:

- If the bandwidth is too small, enough data points may be missed, and convergence might never be reached.
- If the bandwidth is too large, a few clusters may be missed completely.

Q46. There are 2 Types of Hierarchical Clustering. Which one is top-down approach?

a) Agglomerative method

b) Divisive method

Answer: b) Divisive method

There are two main methods for performing hierarchical clustering:

- Agglomerative method: it is a bottom-up approach, in the beginning, we treat every data point as a single cluster. Then, we compute similarity between clusters and merge the two most similar clusters. We repeat the last step until we have a single cluster that contains all data points.
- Divisive method: it is a top-down approach, where we put all data points in a single cluster. Then, we divide this single cluster into two clusters and recursively do the same thing for the two clusters until there is one cluster for every data point. This method is less common than the agglomerative method.

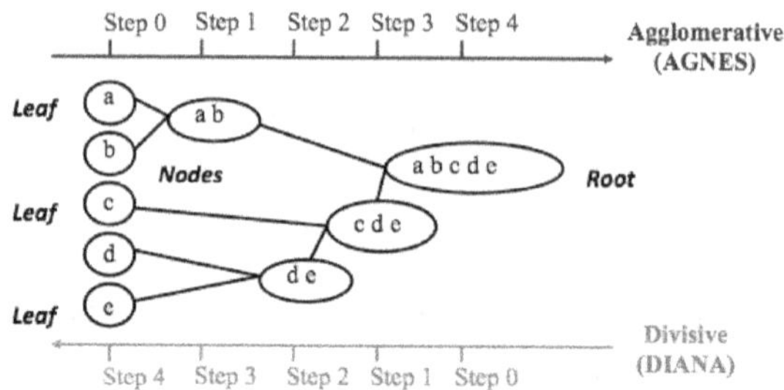

Q47. What is the meaning of homoscedasticity?

a) No outliers

b) Equal variance

c) F-Score = 1

d) Mean within 20%

Answer: b) Equal variance

Homoscedasticity means equal variance.

Q48. Expectation Maximization Clustering is an example of?

a) Hard clustering

b) Soft Clustering

Answer: b) Soft Clustering

Hard clustering means we have non-overlapping clusters, where each instance belongs to one and only one cluster. In a soft clustering method, a single individual can belong to multiple clusters, often with a confidence (belief) associated with each cluster.

Expectation Maximization Clustering is a Soft Clustering method. This means, that it will not form fixed, non-intersecting clusters. There is no rule for one point to belong to

48

one cluster, and one cluster only. In EM Clustering, we talk about probability of each data point to be present in either of the clusters. It is completely possible for multiple clusters to partly share a portion of the data point, since we are only talking about respective probabilities of the point with respect to the clusters.

Q49. For which distribution, one should not use Normalization?

a) Normal Distribution

b) Gaussian Distribution

c) Exponential Distribution

Answer: b) Gaussian Distribution

Normalization is a good technique to use when you do not know the distribution of your data or when you know the distribution

---

is not Gaussian (a bell curve). Normalization
is useful when your data has varied scales
and the algorithm you are using does not
make assumptions about the distribution of
your data, such as k-nearest neighbors and
artificial neural networks.

**Q50. What is the assumption of
Standardization?**

a) Data is uniformly distributed

b) Data is random

c) Data has Gaussian distribution

Answer: c) Data has Gaussian distribution

Standardization assumes that your data has
a Gaussian (bell curve) distribution. This
does not strictly have to be true, but the
technique is more effective if your attribute
distribution is Gaussian. Standardization is

useful when your data has varying scales and the algorithm you are using does make assumptions about your data having a Gaussian distribution, such as linear regression, logistic regression, and linear discriminant analysis.

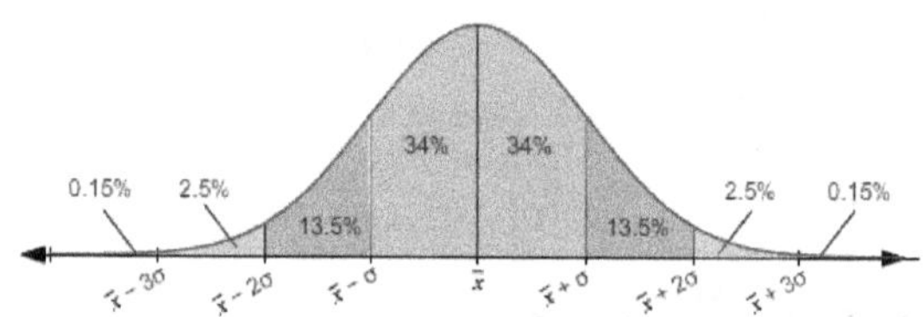

Q51. Which Naive Bayes Classifier has features in binary form?

a) Multinomial Naive Bayes

b) Bernoulli Naive Bayes

c) Gaussian Naive Bayes

Answer: b) Bernoulli Naive Bayes

Bernoulli Naive Bayes is used for discrete data and it works on Bernoulli distribution. The main feature of Bernoulli Naive Bayes is that it accepts features only as binary values like true or false, yes or no, success or failure, 0 or 1 and so on. So when the feature values are binary we know that we have to use Bernoulli Naive Bayes classifier.

Q52. In a Random Decision Forest, what is the n_estimators hyper-parameter?

a) Number of decision trees

b) Degree of randomness

c) Number of features

Answer: a) Number of decision trees

Important Hyperparameters of Random Decision Forest:

- n_estimators: This indicates the number of decision trees we intend to use. Generally, the higher the number of trees, the more accurate will our model be.
- random_state: Since Random Forest uses a considerable degree of randomness in it's approach, our predictions may vary with different random states. We use this for consistency.
- max_features: This helps in increasing the accuracy of our model. It is the maximum number of features to consider when splitting a node.

Q53. Which one of the following is not an ensemble method?

a) Bagging

b) Boosting

c) Stacking

d) None

Answer: d) None

Different Ensemble techniques used in the domain of Machine Learning:

- Bagging
- Boosting
- Stacking

Q54. What is the full form of Bagging ensemble technique?

a) Bayesian-aging

b) Bootstrap Aggregation

c) Bag of Bags

d) None

Answer: b) Bootstrap Aggregation

Bagging, also known as Bootstrap Aggregation is an ensemble technique in which the main idea is to combine the results of multiple models (for instance- say decision trees) to get generalized and better predictions. The critical concept in Bagging technique is Bootstrapping, which is a sampling technique (with replacement) in which we create multiple subsets (also known as bags) of observations using the original data.

Q55. Which ensemble technique uses the concept of weak learners?

a) Bagging

b) Boosting

c) Stacking

Answer: b) Boosting

Boosting is a type of ensemble technique which combines a set of weak learners to form a strong learner. As we saw above, Bagging is based on parallel execution of base learners while on the other hand Boosting is a sequential process, wherein each subsequent model attempts to rectify the errors made by the previous model in the sequence which indicates succeeding models are dependent on the previous model.

The terminology 'weak learner' refers to a model which is slightly better than the random guessing model but nowhere close to a good predictive model. In each iteration, a larger weight is assigned to the points which were misclassified in the previous iteration, such that, they are now predicted correctly. The final output in case of classification is computed using weighted majority vote similarly for regression we use the weighted sum.

Q56. What is Stacking?

a) Stacked Generalization

b) Modified Bagging

Answer: a) Stacked Generalization

Stacking also referred to Stacked Generalization is an ensemble technique which combines predictions from multiple models to create a new model. The new model is termed as meta-learner. In general, Stacking usually provides a better performance compared to any of the single model. The following figure illustrates the Stacking technique:

57

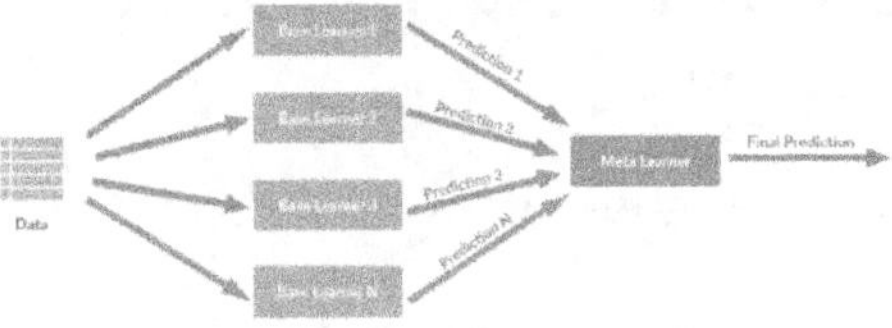

Q57. What is Regression?

a) It is a technique to predict values

b) It is a technique to fix data

c) It is a Machine Learning algorithm

d) It is a technique to find outliers

Answer: a) It is a technique to predict values

Regression is used to create a relationship between a dependent variable to a one or more independent variables.

Q58. What is a dependent variable in Regression?

a) The value we want to predict

b) The features of our dataset

c) The parameters of the regression algorithm

d) The values that interfere in the value we want to predict

Answer: a) The value we want to predict

Dependent variable is the value we want to predict. Imagine that we want to know how much is the value of a house. It is the dependent variable and we have to consider it's size, neighborhood, how many rooms, how many bathrooms, does it have a garden, among other variables. It's value depends of all these information, and that is why it is called Dependent Variable.

Q59. What are independent variables in Regression?

a) The parameters of the regression algorithm

b) The features of our dataset

c) The values that interfere in the value we want to predict

d) The value we want to predict

Answer: c) The values that interfere in the value we want to predict

Following the house price example, all variables that can interfere in the house price can be called as independent variable. House size, neighborhood, how many rooms, when it was built, etc.

Q60. What are outliers?

a) Values that are correlated to each other

b) Extreme datapoints in our dataset

c) It is the main trend of our dataset

d) It is a regression technique

Answer: b) Extreme datapoints in our dataset

Outliers are extreme datapoints in our dataset that have too much more or less value than other datapoints. Most of the times outliers can be excluded from the dataset in order to preserve the regression quality. On the other hand, if we are working to prevent fraud, outliers are what we will be looking for, since they represent suspicious behavior.

Q61. What is Multicollinearity?

a) High correlation between independent variables

b) Low correlation between independent variables

c) Correlation between outliers

d) Correlation between features

Answer: a) High correlation between independent variables

When we have 2 or more independent variables with high correlation, we call it of Multicollinearity. It can be harmful to our regression because make harder to ranking the variables in order to know which one interfere more in our dependent variable. In these cases, we usually keep only one of those variables and discard the others.

Q62. What is overfitting?

a) Great result in training and great result in test

b) Great result in training and poor result in test

c) Poor result in training and poor result in test

d) Poor result in training and poor result in test

Answer: b) Great result in training and poor result in test

When we use unnecessary explanatory variables, it might lead to overfitting.

Q63. What are Linear and Logistic regression?

a) It is how you can classify a regression

b) A regression must be Linear or Logistic

c) There are types of overfittings

d) There are types of regression

Answer: d) There are types of regression

Although they are the most known types of Regression, there are many others.

Q64. Linear Regression is an example of?

a) Supervised Learning

b) Unsupervised Learning

c) Semi-Supervised Learning

Answer: a) Supervised Learning

Linear Regression is an example of Supervised Learning. In fact, as a rule, all Regression techniques are an example of Supervised Learning.

Q65. Logistic Regression is an example of?

a) Supervised Learning: Regression

b) Classification

b) Unsupervised Learning

c) Semi-Supervised Learning

Answer: b) Classification

Logistic Regression is an example of Classification which is a type of Supervised Learning. As mentioned previously, all Regression techniques are an example of Supervised Learning. Exception is that Logistic Regression is not counted as a regression technique but as a Classification technique.

Q66. Which answer explains better Linear Regression?

a) Dependent variable is discrete, independent variable(s) can be continuous or discrete, and nature of regression line is linear.

b) Dependent variable is continuous, independent variable(s) can be continuous or discrete, and nature of regression line is linear.

c) Dependent variable is continuous, independent variable(s) can be continuous or discrete, and nature of regression line is non-linear.

d) Dependent variable is discrete, independent variable(s) can be continuous or discrete, and nature of regression line is non-linear.

Answer: b) Dependent variable is continuous, independent variable(s) can be continuous or discrete, and nature of regression line is linear.

Linear Regression creates a relation between the dependent variables and all the independent variables using a best fit straight line, known as regression line.

Q67. When is appropriate to use Logistic Regression?

a) When the independent variables are binary

b) When the dependent variable is not binary

c) When the dependent variable is binary

d) When the independent variables are not binary

Answer: c) When the dependent variable is binary

Logistic Regression is used when we are looking for a binary value. This type of regression calculates the probability of a event has success or failure. It is widely used for classification.

Q68. For what Polynomial Regression is used?

a) Handle linear and separable data

---

b) Handle with non-linear and separable data

c) Classify binary data

d) Find the best linear line

Answer: b) Handle with non-linear and separable data

When we handle with non-linear and separable data, a straight line will not work. In this case, Polynomial is very useful and their always have independents variables with power higher than 1.

Q69. When we use Ridge Regression?

a) When our data have multicollinearity

b) When our data does not have multicollinearity

c) When we have a lot of outliers

d) When there is no outlier

Answer: a) When our data have multicollinearity

Ridge Regression have a regularization parameter to fix the multicollinearity problem. It shrinks the value of coefficients but doesn't reaches zero, which suggests no feature selection feature.

Q70. Which regression is used in the following image?

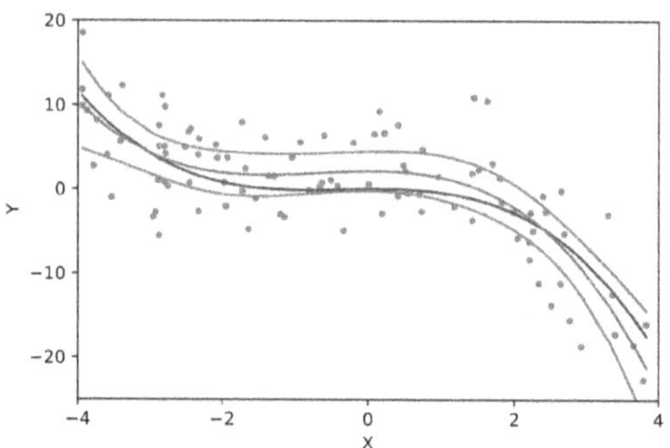

a) Linear Regression

b) Logistic Regression

c) Polynomial Regression

d) Ridge Regression

Answer: c) Polynomial Regression

Multiple curves in a line denote the graph is of a polynomial of multiple degree and hence, it is using Polynomial Regression.

Q71. Which way Lasso Regression differs from Ridge Regression?

a) It uses square values in regularization parameter

b) It uses absolute values in regularization parameter, instead of squares

c) It works better in small datasets

d) It works better in big datasets

Answer: b) It uses absolute values in regularization parameter, instead of squares

Lasso Regression uses absolute values in the penalty function, instead of squares. The result is penalized values which causes some of the parameter estimates to turn out exactly zero.

Q72. What is ElasticNet Regression?

a) It is a mix of Lasso and Ridge Regression

b) It is the newest type of regression

c) It is the best way to use regression in Machine Learning

d) It is a type of regression focused in outliers

Answer: a) It is a mix of Lasso and Ridge Regression

It is a combination of L1 and L2 regularization.

Q73. Consider the following image. Which one is used for Low Bias Low Variance?

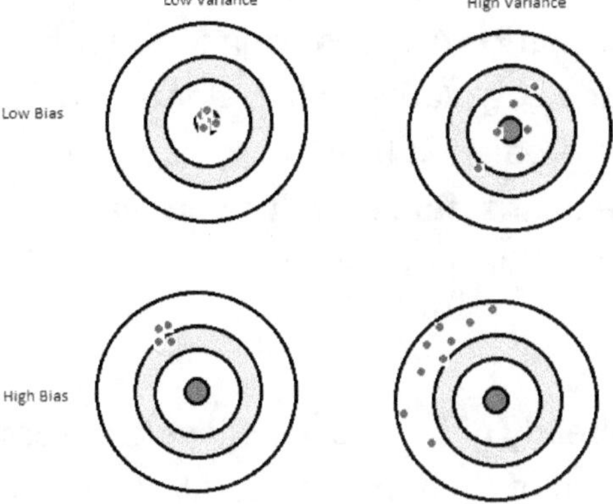

a) Ridge Regression

b) Lasso Regression

c) Elastic Net Regression

d) Linear Regression

___

Answer: c) Elastic Net Regression

Ridge and Lasso Regression is used for high bias and high variance.

The scenario we are looking for is with Low Bias and Low Variance in order to have a better prediction from our model. Then we use regularization to reduce our variance and introducing some Bias.

We already did that using Ridge and Lasso, but both of them has faults. Elastic Net was created to combine the penalties of ridge regression and lasso to get the best of both worlds. Elastic Net aims at minimizing the loss information.

Q74. Which Regression technique uses F-test or T-test?

a) Ridge Regression

b) Stepwise Regression

c) Elastic Net Regression

d) Linear Regression

Answer: b) Stepwise Regression

Stepwise regression is a technique which adds or removes variables via series of F-tests or T-tests. The variables to be added or removed are chosen based on the test statistics of the estimated coefficients.

Q75. Principal Component Analysis (PCA) is an example of?

a) Supervised Learning

b) Unsupervised Learning

c) Semi-Supervised Learning

Answer: b) Unsupervised Learning

Principal Component Analysis (PCA) is an example of Unsupervised Learning. Moreover, PCA is a dimension reduction technique hence, it is a type of Association in terms of Unsupervised Learning. It can be viewed as a clustering technique as well as it groups common features in an image as separate dimensions.

Q76. What is the importance of using PCA before the clustering? Choose the most complete answer.

a) Find which dimension of data maximize the features variance

b) Find good features to improve your clustering score

c) Avoid bad features

d) Find the explained variance

Answer: a) Find which dimension of data maximize the features variance

In order to improve your clustering efficiency, you need to find which dimension of data maximize the features variance, also with the result you can find the explained variance for each dimension. As more variance you have, less data you loss.

Q77. Following the steps to run a PCA's algorithm, why is so important standardize your data?

a) Standardize data allows other people understand better your work

b) Use the best practices of data wrangling

c) Find the features which can best predicts Y

d) Make the training time more fast

Answer: c) Find the features which can best predicts Y

When you standardize your data, you will find the features with higher variance, and in this case, features that will better predicts our target (y).

Q78. What PCA does after fall?

a) Reduce dimensionality of the data and create new features from features set given

b) Predicts your target with high efficiency

c) Create clusters in order to let you know what are the class

d) Give you the highest number of features possible, to maximize the efficiency of your Machine Learning algorithm

---

Answer: a) Reduce dimensionality of the data and create new features from features set given

With a reduced dimensionality it is easier to visualize your data using a clustering method, will help you to reduce noise from your data and the training phase will be faster.

Q79. Why you have to drop unimportant features?

a) Standardize the data

b) Using the most important features will give you better efficiency predicting your target

c) Find the correct clusters

d) To trains the model faster

Answer: b) Using the most important features will give you better efficiency predicting your target

Using only the most important features will give you an environment with less data loss, will let you know exactly which features is most important and will reduce dimensionality. All of this are the real purpose of PCA.

Q80. When one uses PCA?

a) Every time before uses a Machine Learning algorithm

b) When I have a overfit case

c) You want to find latent features and reduce dimensionality

d) When my data is small and with a few features

Answer: c) You want to find latent features and reduce dimensionality

PCA helps you to find latent features among all your data, can reduce your dimensionality for 1/10, making easier to visualize data and faster training because uses less hardware to run.

Basic Questions from Deep Learning for ML

Q81. The Convolution Layer is what makes CNN so powerful. How this layer operates?

a) Conv Layer has a big database of features which can gather information to find the best output

b) Conv Layer has parameters that consists in learnable filters, each one being small spatially but extends through the full depth of the input volume

c) Conv Layer has parameters that consists in how much iterations you want do to

d) Analyzing the features considering their input volume

Answer: b) Conv Layer has parameters that consists in learnable filters, each one being

---

small spatially but extends through the full depth of the input volume

After the filter expansion, intuitively, the network will learn filters that activate when they see some type of visual feature such as an edge of some orientation or a blotch of some color on the first layer.

Q82. What is the receptive field?

a) Is the name given to the connectivity of neurons only to a local region of the input volume

b) Is the name given to the relationship of neurons

c) Is the name given to the connectivity of neurons only to a local region of the output volume

d) It happens when neurons has difficult to find connections, and this hyperparameters helps it

Answer: a) Is the name given to the connectivity of neurons only to a local region of the input volume

When dealing with high-dimensional inputs such as images, it is impractical to connect neurons to all neurons in the previous volume.

Q83. Which answer explains better the hyperparameter Depth?

a) It corresponds of how deep the connections between neurons will be

b) It corresponds to the number of features we would like to use, each learning to look for something different in the input

c) It corresponds to the number of filters we would like to use, each learning to look for something different in the input

d) It corresponds to the number of features we would like to use, each learning to look for something different in the previous output

---

Answer: c) It corresponds to the number of filters we would like to use, each learning to look for something different in the input

For example, if the first Convolutional Layer takes as input the raw image, then different neurons along the depth dimension may activate in presence of various oriented edges, or blobs of color. We will refer to a set of neurons that are all looking at the same region of the input as a depth column.

Q84. Which answer explains better the hyperparameter Stride?

a) It is how much pixels, filters will be moved

b) It is how much filters, pixels will be moved

c) It is how much features will be used

d) It defines how many outputs we will receive

Answer: a) It is how much pixels, filters will be moved

When our strider is 1, filters will move 1 pixel at a time. If our strider is 2, it will move 2 pixels at a time. Sometimes stride is 3 or more, but it is unusual.

Q85. Which answer explains better the hyperparameter Zero-padding?

a) It pads the missing values with zero

b) It says how many zeros you use to pad the input volume

c) It avoids zero between the values

d) It says how many zeros you use to pad the output volume

Answer: b) It says how many zeros you use to pad the input volume

Sometimes pad the input volumes with zeros in the border help us to control spatial size of the output volumes.

Q86. What is feature map in Convolutional Layer?

a) It is a map of features learned by the CNN

b) It is a map of features that you use as input

---

c) It is a map of features that helps CNN to make better predictions

d) If is a map of features that the algorithm will not use

Answer: a) It is a map of features learned by the CNN

Every time CNN finds an important feature, it is stored in feature map. Also, if we have a combination of features in a certain area, its possible that we have a more important and complex feature there.

Q87. When we are talking about Conv Layer, what is Kernel Size?

a) Kernel size = n_inputs / n_outputs

b) Kernel size = (2 * n_inputs) * n_outputs

c) Kernel size = n_inputs * (2 * n_outputs)

---

d) Kernel size = n_inputs * n_outputs

Answer: d) Kernel size = n_inputs * n_outputs

A fully connected layer connects every input with every output in his kernel term.

Q88. Why is so important to keep Kernel Size small?

a) The number of parameters grows quadratically with kernel size.

b) The number of features grows quadratically with kernel size.

c) The number of parameters decreases quadratically with kernel size.

d) The number of features decreases quadratically with kernel size.

Answer: a) The number of parameters grows quadratically with kernel size.

This makes big convolution kernels not cost efficient enough, even more, when we want a big number of channels.

Q89. What is the Kernel Size more used nowadays?

a) 3x3 and 5x5

b) 3x3 and 9x9

c) 5x5 and 7x7

d) 5x5 and 11x11

Answer: a) 3x3 and 5x5

Those Kernel Sizes provides a good result costing less.

Q90. Conv Layers are powerful but also has big computational cost. Which of the techniques below can make it cheaper?

a) Bigger Convolutions

b) Smaller Convolutions

c) Wider Convolutions

d) Faster Convolutions

Answer: c) Wider Convolutions

In Wider Convolutions we use less but fatter layers, where fat means more kernels per layer. It's easier for the GPU, or other massively parallel machines for that matter, to process a single big chunk of data instead of a lot of smaller ones.

Q91. What is the Fully Connected Layer?

---

a) It is the last layer of CNN

b) It is the phase that generates the output

c) It is the first layer of CNN

d) It is the phase that all layers are connected

Answer: b) It is the phase that generates the output

FC layer looks at what high level features most strongly correlate to a particular class and has particular weights so that when you compute the products between the weights and the previous layer, you get the correct probabilities for the different classes.

Q92. What does it mean if Fully Connected layer gives us this output: [.15, .15, .60, .10]

a) It means how many iterations we did so far

b) It says how many features we used

c) It says the probability of of each class

d) FC does not give us this kind of output

Answer: c) It says the probability of each class.

For this output, FC is saying to us that the first and second class has 15% of probability. Third class has 60% of probability and fourth class has 10%.

Q93. How Fully Connected layer operates?

a) Detects an input and generates a output

b) Generates outputs according to the features

c) Detects an output and generates a input

d) Generates inputs according to the features

Answer: a) Detects an input and generates a output

This layer basically takes an input volume (whatever the output is of the conv or ReLU or pool layer preceding it) and outputs an N dimensional vector where N is the number of classes that the program has to choose from.

Q94. Considering the image below, which number represents Fully Connected layer?

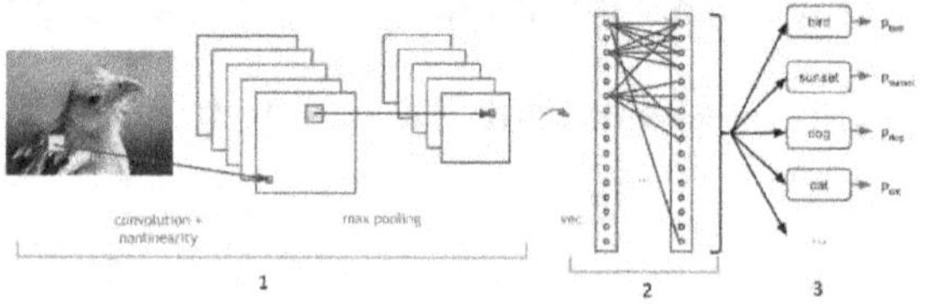

a) 1

b) 2

c) 3

d) None

Answer: b) 2

We can see after Conv and Pooling layers, FC come and provides our output.

Q95. Can Fully Connected layer be used without Conv Layer?

a) Yes

b) No

c) Only with text

d) Only with images

Answer: a) Yes

FC layer can be used without the Conv Layer. The biggest differential from CNN is the Conv Layer that is much more specialized and can discover more and more complex features. Then comes FC to analyse these samplings generated but Conv layers and then creates the output. Without the Conv Layer, FC could be used just fine, but in complex cases like images, it would not be so efficient.

Q96. Why Conv Layers are not replaced by Fully Connected layers?

a) Performance

b) Accuracy

c) Conv Layers can be replaced by FC Layers

d) Computationally Expensiveness

Answer: d) Computationally Expensiveness

Fully Connected Layers appears only at the end of CNN for a reason. Depending on the size of what you are analyzing, you will have too much parameters, increasing the cost and resources needed. Conv Layer reduces it to the most important features, keeping the efficiency considerable.

Q97. How much time is consumed by Fully Connected layer in a Machine Learning model in general?

a) 5%

b) 10%

c) 30%

d) 70%

Answer: b) 10%

Overall, 10% Inference time is consumed by Fully Connected layer. The most computationally intensive operation is Convolution taking up to 70% of Inference time.

Q98. What is the time complexity of Fully Connected layer in a Machine Learning model for a 3D image?

a) O(D*W*H*N)

b) O(H*W)

c) $O(H^2 * W^2)$

d) O(W*H*N)

Answer: a) O(D*W*H*N)

The time complexity of Fully Connected layer is O(D*W*H*N) where:

- D = Channel of input
- W = Width of input
- H = Height of input
- N = batch size of input.

Q99. What can be done by a Fully Connected layer?

a) Feature extraction

b) Classification

c) Dimension reduction

d) Feature detection

Answer: b) Classification

After feature extraction in a Machine Learning model, we need to classify the data into various classes, this can be done using a fully connected (FC) neural network.

Q100. In TensorFlow v2.x, Fully Connected layer (tf.contrib.layers.fully_connected()) has been removed. How to use it now?

a) tf.layers.fully_connected()

b) tf.fully_connected()

c) tf.layers.Dense

d) tf.keras.layers.Dense

Answer: d) tf.keras.layers.Dense

In TensorFlow v2.x, tf.contrib has been removed. Fully connected layers can be used with tf.keras.layers.Dense but you need to use Keras API.

Q101. For which purpose Convolutional Neural Network is used?

a) It is a multi-purpose algorithm that can be used for Unsupervised Learning.

b) Mainly to process and analyze digital images, with some success cases involving processing voice and natural language.

c) Mainly to process and analyze financial models, predicting future trends.

d) It is a multi-purpose algorithm that can be used for Supervised Learning.

Answer: b) Mainly to process and analyze digital images, with some success cases involving processing voice and natural language.

CNN has some components and parameters which works well with images. That's why

102

---

it´s mainly used to analyze and predict images.

Q102. What is the biggest advantage utilizing CNN?

a) It is easy to understand and fast to implement.

b) It has the highest accuracy among all algorithms that predicts images.

c) Little dependence on preprocessing, decreasing the needs of human effort developing its functionalities.

d) It works well both for Supervised and Unsupervised Learning.

Answer: c) Little dependence on preprocessing, decreasing the needs of human effort developing its functionalities.

With little dependence on preprocessing, this algorithm requires less human effort. It is actually a self-learner, which makes the preprocessing phase, easier.

Convolutional Neural Network has 5 basic components: Convolution, ReLU, Pooling, Flattening and Full Connection. Based on this information, please answer the questions below.

Q103. Which answer explains better the Convolution?

a) It is the first step to use CNN.

b) Understand the model features and selecting the best.

c) It is a technique to standardize the dataset.

d) Detect key features in images, respecting their spatial boundaries.

Answer: d) Detect key features in images, respecting their spatial boundaries.

This is the component which detect features in images preserving the relationship between pixels by learning image features using small squares of input data.

Q104. Which answer explains better the ReLU?

a) It is used to find the best features considering their correlation.

b) Helps in the detection of features, increasing the non-linearity of the image, converting positive pixels to zero. This behavior allows you to detect variations of attributes.

c) Helps in the detection of features, decreasing the non-linearity of the image, converting negative pixels to zero. This behavior allows you to detect variations of attributes.

d) A technique that allows you to find outliers.

Answer: c) Helps in the detection of features, decreasing the non-linearity of the image, converting negative pixels to zero. This behavior allows you to detect variations of attributes.

Usually a image is highly non-linear, which means varied pixel values. This is a scenario that is very difficult to an algorithm makes correct predictions. ReLU comes to decrease the non-linearity and make the job easier.

Q105. Which answer explains better the Pooling?

---

a) It assists in the detection of distorted features, in order to find dominant attributes.

b) It assists in the detection of features, even if they are distorted, in addition to decreasing the attribute sizes, resulting in decreased computational need. It is also very useful for extracting dominant attributes.

c) Creates a pool of data in order to improve the accuracy of the algorithm predicting images.

d) Decrease the features size, in order to decrease the computational power that are needed.

Answer: b) It assists in the detection of features, even if they are distorted, in addition to decreasing the attribute sizes, resulting in decreased computational need. It is also very useful for extracting dominant attributes.

As a result of pooling, even if the picture were a little tilted, the largest number in a certain region of the feature map would have been recorded and hence, the feature would have been preserved. Also, as another benefit, reducing the size by a very significant amount will uses less computational power.

Q106. Which answer explains better the Flattening?

a) Transform images to vectors to make it easier to predict.

b) Delete unnecessary features to make our dataset cleaner.

c) It is the last step of CNN.

d) Once we have the pooled feature map, this component transforms the information into a vector. It's the input we need to get on with Artificial Neural Networks.

Answer: d) Once we have the pooled feature map, this component transforms the information into a vector. It's the input we need to get on with Artificial Neural Networks.

In the flattening procedure, we basically take the elements in a pooled feature map and put them in a vector form. This becomes the input layer for the upcoming ANN.

Q107. Which answer explains better the Full Connection?

a) Full Connection acts by placing different weights in each synapse in order to minimize errors. This step can be repeated until an expected result is achieved.

b) Full Connection acts by placing different weights in each synapse in order to minimize errors. No iteration is needed, since we can get the best results in our first attempt.

c) It is the last step of CNN, where we connect the results of the earlier components to create a output.

d) It is a component that connects different algorithms in order to increase the accuracy.

Answer: a) Full Connection acts by placing different weights in each synapse in order to minimize errors. This step can be repeated until an expected result is achieved.

It works like a ANN, assigning random weights to each synapse, the input layer is weight adjusted and put into an activation function. The output of this is then compared to the true values and the error generated is back-propagated, that is the weights are re-adjusted and all the processes repeated. This is done until the error or cost function is minimized.

Q108. What are the Pooling Types? What are their characteristics?

a) Max Pooling and Average Pooling. Max pooling returns the maximum value of the portion covered by the kernel, while Average pooling returns the measure of that portion and suppresses the Noises.

b) Max Pooling and Minimum Pooling. Max pooling returns the maximum value of the portion covered by the kernel and suppresses the Noises, while Minimum pooling only returns the smallest value of that portion.

c) Max Pooling and Average Pooling. Max pooling returns the maximum value of the portion covered by the kernel and suppresses the Noises, while Average pooling only returns the measure of that portion.

d) Max Pooling and Std Pooling. Max pooling returns the maximum value of the portion covered by the kernel, while Std Pooling returns the standard deviation of that portion.

Answer: c) Max Pooling and Average Pooling. Max pooling returns the maximum value of the portion covered by the kernel and suppresses the Noises, while Average pooling only returns the measure of that portion.

It is recommended to use Max Pooling most of the time.

Q109. CNN is divided in two big steps. Feature Learning and Classification. What happens in each step?

a) Feature Learning has Convolution, ReLU and Pooling components, with numerous iterations between them before move to Classification, which uses the Flattening and Full Connection components.

b) Feature Learning has Flattening and Full Connection components, with numerous iterations between them before move to Classification, which uses the Convolution, ReLU and Pooling components.

c) During Feature Learning, CNN uses appropriates algorithms to it, while during classification its changes the algorithm in order to achieve the expected result.

Answer: a) Feature Learning has Convolution, ReLU and Pooling components, with inumerous iterations between them before move to Classification, which uses the Flattening and Full Connection components.

During Feature Learning, the algorithm is learning about it's dataset. Components like Convolution, ReLU and Pooling works for that. Once the features are known, the classification happens using the Flattening and Full Connection components.

Q110. What is the difference between CNN and ANN?

a) CNN uses a more simpler algorithm than ANN.

b) CNN is a easiest way to use Neural Networks.

c) They complete each other, so in order to use ANN, you need to start with CNN.

d) CNN has one or more layers of convolution units, which receives its input from multiple units.

Answer: d) CNN has one or more layers of convolution units, which receives its input from multiple units.

The only difference is the Convolutional component, which is what makes CNN good in analyzing and predict data like images. The other steps are the same.

Q111. What is the benefit to use CNN instead ANN?

a) Increase the number of units in the network, which means more parameters to learn and increase chance of overfitting. Also, they consider the context information in the small neighborhoods. This feature is very important to achieve a better prediction.

b) Reduce the number of units in the network, which means fewer parameters to learn and reduced chance of overfitting. Also they consider the context information in the small neighborhoods. This feature is very important to achieve a better prediction in data like images.

c) There is no benefit, ANN is always better.

d) CNN has better results since you have more computational power.

Answer: b) Reduce the number of units in the network, which means fewer parameters to learn and reduced chance of overfitting. Also, they consider the context information in the small neighborhoods. This feature is very important to achieve a better prediction in data like images.

Since digital images are a bunch of pixels with high values, makes sense use CNN to analyze them. CNN decrease their values, which is better for training phase with less computational power and less information loss.

Q112. What 'Shared Weights' means in CNN?

a) It is what makes CNN 'convolutional'. Forcing the neurons of one layer to share weights, the forward pass becomes the equivalent of convolving a filter over the image to produce a new image. Then the training phase become a task of learning filters, deciding what features you should look for in the data.

b) Sharing weights among the features, make it easier and faster to CNN predict the correct image.

c) It means that CNN use the weights of each feature in order to find the best model to make prediction, sharing the results and returning the average.

d) It calculates the feature´s weights and compare with other algorithms in order to find the best parameters.

Answer: a) It is what makes CNN 'convolutional'. Forcing the neurons of one layer to share weights, the forward pass becomes the equivalent of convolving a filter over the image to produce a new image. Then the training phase become a task of learning filters, deciding what features you should look for in the data.

This feature is what makes CNN better to analyze images than ANN. The Convolutional component of CNN simplify the images structures and the algorithm can predict better.

RNN questions

Q113. What is the basic concept of Recurrent Neural Network?

a) Use a loop between inputs and outputs in order to achieve the better prediction.

b) Use previous inputs to find the next output according to the training set.

c) Use recurrent features from dataset to find the best answers.

d) Use loops between the most important features to predict next output.

Answer: b) Use previous inputs to find the next output according to the training set.

After you train your RNN algorithm, it calculates the Output according to your input. Important to say, is that it calculates input after input, so if you have 2 inputs or more, it calculates the first output and consider it as next input to calculate next output.

Q114. For what RNN is used and achieve the best results?

a) Handwriting and speech recognition

b) Handwriting and images recognition

c) Speech and images recognition

d) Financial predictions

Answer: a) Handwriting and speech recognition

Due it´s behavior, RNN is great to recognize handwriting and speech, calculating each input (letter/word or a second of a audio file for example), to find the correct outputs. Basically, RNN was made to process information sequences.

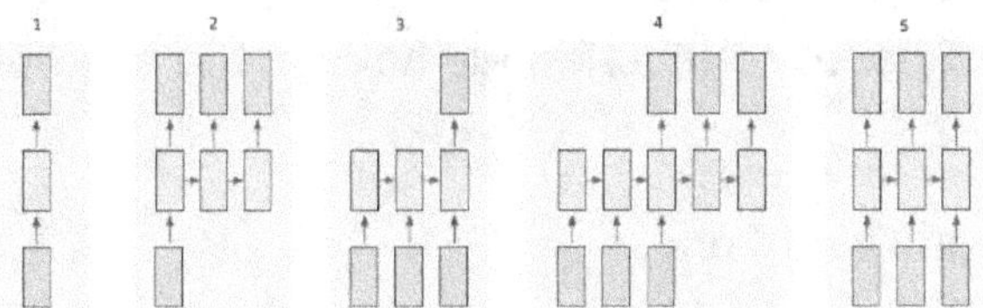

Q115. According to the image, classify the type of connection we have in the example 1.

a) One to one

b) One to many

c) Many to one

d) Many to many

Answer: a) One to one

In the one-to-one case we have the classic feedforward neural network.

Q116. According to the image, classify the type of connection we have in the example 2.

a) One to one

b) One to many

c) Many to one

d) Many to many

Answer: b) One to many

In one-to-many applications, we read the data only once for the hidden state, and then we pass that hidden state forward for various periods of time, in which we also read information contained in it. An example of such an application is when we want to create a model for describing images. In this case, we read the image once to the hidden state, but we read of that hidden state several times, once for each word generated in the image description.

Q117. According to the image, classify the type of connection we have in the example 3.

a) One to one

b) One to many

c) Many to one

d) Many to many

Answer: c) Many to one

In the many to one case, we read the data several times, but we produce a forecast only after reading the whole sequence. A good example of this type of application is text classification, such as analysis of feelings, where we read the whole text before making a prediction.

Q118. According to the image, classify the type of connection we have in the example 4.

a) One to one

b) One to many

c) Many to one

d) Many to many

Answer: d) Many to many

In this case of many to many applications, we read the data for a few periods of time before we start releasing forecasts. In other words, there is a discrepancy between the reading of the input sequence and the output of the output sequence. An example of such applications are cases of machine translation or audio transcription, where the RNR reads the sequence for some time before starting to generate the output sequence, be it the words in another language or the words corresponding to an audio.

Q119. According to the image, classify the type of connection we have in the example 5.

a) One to one

b) One to many

c) Many to one

d) Many to many

Answer: d) Many to many

In this case of many to many applications is when we have sequences in the input and output of the network, but each input corresponds to an output in the same time period. This type of data structure appears in time series and dashboard data, in which we want to make a forecast for the next time period, given what has occurred in this time period and in previous periods.

Q120. What is 'gradient' when we are talking about RNN?

a) A gradient is a partial derivative with respect to its inputs

b) It is how RNN calls it´s features

c) The most important step of RNN algorithm

d) A parameter that can help you improve the algorithm's accuracy

---

Answer: a) A gradient is a partial derivative with respect to its inputs

A gradient measure how much the output of a function changes, if you change the inputs a little bit.

The higher the gradient, the steeper the slope and the faster a model can learn. But if the slope is zero, the model stops to learning. A gradient simply measures the change in all weights with regard to the change in error.

Q121. One of the RNN´s issue is 'Exploding Gradients'. What is that?

---

a) When the algorithm assigns a stupidly high importance to the weights, because the better features

b) When the algorithm assigns a stupidly high importance to the weights, when your dataset is too big

c) When the algorithm assigns a stupidly high importance to the weights, when your data is too small

d) When the algorithm assigns a stupidly high importance to the weights, without much reason

---

Answer: d) When the algorithm assigns a stupidly high importance to the weights, without much reason

This problem can be easily solved if you truncate or squash the gradients.

Q122. The other RNN´s issue is called 'Vanishing Gradients'. What is that?

a) When the values of a gradient are too big and the model stops learning or takes way too long because of that.

b) When the values of a gradient are too small and the model joins in a loop because of that.

c) When the values of a gradient are too small and the model stops learning or takes way too long because of that.

d) When the values of a gradient are too big and the model joins in a loop because of that.

Answer: c) When the values of a gradient are too small and the model stops learning or takes way too long because of that.

128

This was a major problem in the 1990s and much harder to solve than the exploding gradients. Fortunately, it was solved through the concept of LSTM by Sepp Hochreiter and Juergen Schmidhuber.

Q123. LSTM? What is that?

a) LSTM networks are an extension for recurrent neural networks, which basically extends their memory. Therefore, it is well suited to learn from important experiences that have very long-time lags in between

b) LSTM networks are an extension for recurrent neural networks, which basically extends their memory. Therefore, it is well suited to learn from important experiences that have very low time lags in between

c) LSTM networks are an extension for recurrent neural networks, which basically shorten their memory. Therefore, it is well suited to learn from important experiences that have very low time lags in between

d) LSTM networks are an extension for recurrent neural networks, which basically extends their memory. Therefore, it is not recommended to use it, unless you are using a small Dataset.

Answer: a) LSTM networks are an extension for recurrent neural networks, which basically extends their memory. Therefore, it is well suited to learn from important experiences that have very long-time lags in between.

The units of an LSTM are used as building units for the layers of a RNN, which is then often called an LSTM network.

LSTM's enable RNN's to remember their inputs over a long period of time. This is because LSTM's contain their information in a memory, that is much like the memory of a computer because the LSTM can read, write and delete information from its memory.

With this, you must have a solid practice of Machine Learning Interview questions. If you got any question wrong, dive deeper into the topic and get well prepared for Machine Learning Interview.

For more practice and contribute to Computing
Community, feel free to join our Internship
Program: **internship.OPENGENUS.org**

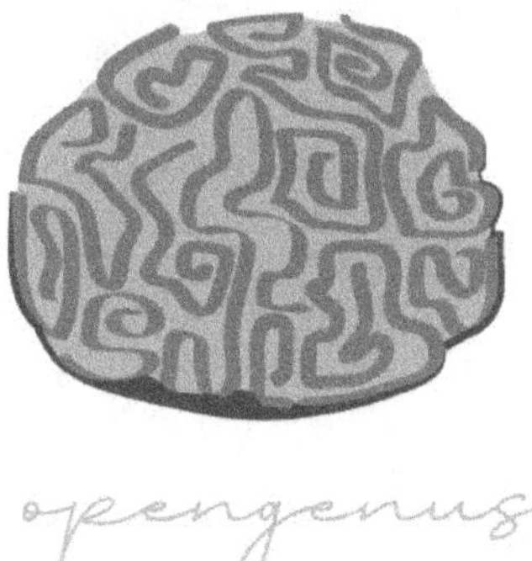